DOCTOR WHO MEMORABILIA

An Unofficial Guide to *Doctor Who* Collectables

Paul Berry

AMBERLEY

Acknowledgements

The author would like to thank the following people for their help on this book: Mark Stone, Adam Lonsdale, Marc Thorpe, Dale Santos, Mark Worgan, David Wilson and Ian Philip Snell.

First published 2017

Amberley Publishing
The Hill, Stroud
Gloucestershire, GL5 4EP

www.amberley-books.com

Copyright © Paul Berry, 2017

The right of Paul Berry to be identified as the Author of this work has been asserted in accordance with the Copyrights, Designs and Patents Act 1988.

ISBN 978 1 4456 6552 8 (print)
ISBN 978 1 4456 6553 5 (ebook)

British Library Cataloguing in Publication Data.
A catalogue record for this book is available from the British Library.

Typesetting by Amberley Publishing.
Printed in the UK.

Contents

Introduction

Doctor Who was first broadcast in the UK on 23 November 1963. It arrived with little fanfare, even though it was an ambitious series, which it was hoped would run for a year, and was designed to break new boundaries in technical achievements for the British Broadcasting Corporation.

Although the BBC had commercially exploited some of its characters before, such as *Bill and Ben* and *Andy Pandy*, its licensing division comprised only one staff member, and faith in the programme was such that no real thought had been given to merchandising this new science fiction series.

Overshadowed by the assassination of President Kennedy the previous day, *Doctor Who*'s first episode, 'An Unearthly Child', attracted modest if not fantastic ratings, and it wasn't until four weeks later, when the TARDIS landed on the desolate world of Skaro, that the programme really began to take off. It was here that viewers were introduced to a new alien race – the Daleks. Ratings began to climb and the BBC was besieged by letters from viewers wanting to know more about these robot-like creatures and when they would be back, while manufacturers quickly saw their inherent marketing potential.

Initial products were slow out of the gate, with only a small amount of items in store for the creatures' return to television screens just before Christmas 1964. However, by mid-1965 the operation was in full swing and, buoyed by the release of the *Dr. Who & the Daleks* cinema film, the country was swamped with a wave of what is now affectionately termed 'Dalekmania'. Daleks featured on everything from toys and games to sweets and soap. During these early years one could be forgiven for forgetting that the Daleks still formed only a relatively small portion of the Doctor's adventures on television, and items featuring anything non-Dalek related from the series were uncommon.

Like many fads, Dalekmania fizzled out quickly and, by the time the First Doctor, played by William Hartnell, was bowing out of the series, the amount of *Doctor Who* and Dalek products on the market had declined dramatically. The arrival of a new Doctor, in the form of Patrick Troughton, saw the series taking on a relatively low profile, with the amount of licensed products released during the remainder of the 1960s slumping to single figures. This was to continue into the early 1970s; as Jon Pertwee became the Third Doctor and the series moved from black and white into colour, relatively few products were available for the budding enthusiast to buy.

In 1973, *Doctor Who* turned ten years old and had been on television long enough for a generation to grow up with it; this burgeoning fan base was eager to know more about the series history. The previous year had seen a book published on *The Making of* Doctor Who, which was the first bona fide guide to the programme. This was soon

followed by a special magazine published by the *Radio Times*, which celebrated a decade of the series. The tenth-anniversary year also saw the start of one of *Doctor Who* merchandising's biggest success stories – the Target book range. The books, which retold the Doctor's television adventures in print, would run for over twenty years.

As Tom Baker became the fourth actor to play the role in 1974, the series' profile continued to climb and a renewed period of success in the ratings also meant increased interest from toy and novelty manufacturers. While not reaching the height of Dalekmania, the Doctor was to be found once again on a plethora of high street products. The end of the 1970s saw the Doctor finally get his own publication, *Doctor Who Weekly*, after nearly two decades of featuring as a back-up comic strip in television-themed anthology titles.

The 1980s saw a shift in the fortunes of *Doctor Who* merchandising. With Peter Davison in the lead the series was now nearing its twentieth anniversary and many who had been children when William Hartnell had graced screens were now in their mid-twenties. With a larger disposable income these fans demanded a more focused product. Small cottage industry firms started to spring up, mostly run by fans of the series, with products aimed squarely at the collector.

In 1985, *Doctor Who* was dealt a serious blow when production of the twenty-third season of the show was cancelled and postponed until the following year. It was the first attempt by the top brass at the BBC to get rid of what they considered to be an ailing series that was past its prime. When the show did return eighteen months later, it did so to some of the lowest ratings in many years and marked a turbulent period for the programme as the Sixth Doctor – Colin Baker – was dropped from the series.

Sylvester McCoy was to be the final of the classic series' Doctors and, while the series ratings on television were a fraction of what they had been in Tom Baker's heyday, merchandise still sold strongly. Indeed, it was often claimed it generated more revenue

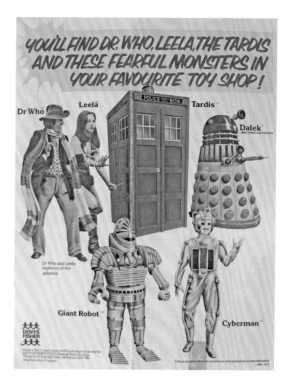

in sales than the series cost to make. When the BBC announced in 1989 that the series would be taking an indefinite break, the merchandising became a lifeline for the fans. While no new episodes were being shown on television, a steady stream of older episodes began to arrive on video, episodes many fans had not seen in decades. Books and comic strips picked up the story of the Doctor's ongoing adventures. Five years after it had been dropped from the television schedules, the series merchandising remained as strong as ever. There was a brief glimmer of hope for many fans when a television movie aired in 1996 starring Paul McGann as the Eighth Doctor. Sadly, although it didn't lead to an ongoing series, it provided a brief shot in the arm for the merchandising, which continued on barely hindered by the lack of a series.

Doctor Who of course returned to television in 2005 and spawned a whole new wave of merchandise, the volume of which now dwarfs that released during the show's first four decades. Due to the sheer amount of product and the fact that, being so recent, much of it is still relatively common and therefore not hugely collectable, the decision was taken to keep this book's focus on the merchandise released up until 2004, which neatly encompasses the first Eight Doctors. Some post-2004 products have been included, but only because they relate to the series' classic era. The post-2005 era and the merchandising story of the Ninth to the Twelfth Doctors is perhaps a story for another time.

This book is by no means intended as a complete guide; in fact, if it were, it would be almost instantly out of date. Here we feature some of the more noteworthy and collectable items with a particular focus on the series' first three decades; so, sit back and enjoy this journey through the story of a television and merchandising phenomenon.

CHAPTER 1

The Books

Doctor Who has enjoyed a long association with books and spin-off fiction. In fact, it could be argued that the printed word is *Doctor Who*'s second home. In the early days, before home video recorders, when episodes would be broadcast once and then vanish into history, the books provided the only way to relive the episodes again. Later, when the BBC halted production of the series, the Doctor seamlessly transferred his adventures to the printed page, where he enjoyed an unbroken fourteen-year run of brand-new stories. *Doctor Who* also boasts an extensive library of factual books covering every aspect of the making of the series.

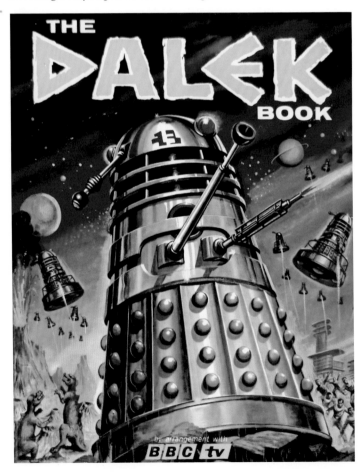

The Dalek Book (Souvenir Press, 1964).

A particular British tradition is the annual, a large hardback book for children released in early autumn for the Christmas market and perplexingly always dated one year ahead of its publication date. One of the earliest examples of merchandising for the series was *The Dalek Book*. The annual-format book did not feature any characters from the programme apart from the Daleks, although it did include a short photographic story utilising stills from the very first Dalek television episode. Two further books followed over the next two years: *The Dalek Oracle* and *The Dalek Outer Space Book*.

The Doctor himself would not feature in an annual until the following year. The 1965 *Doctor Who* annual began a virtually unbroken run of yearly volumes from the Manchester-based World Distributors that would continue for the next twenty years.

Two volumes were issued for William Hartnell, with three for Patrick Troughton and four for Jon Pertwee, while Tom Baker had a record seven volumes; Peter Davison and Colin Baker had two apiece (although a few Davison stories appeared in Tom Baker's last volume). No annual was published in 1971, as the publishers opted to have a gap year following poor sales of the previous two annuals. World also issued four Dalek annuals in the 1970s as well as a K9 annual to tie in with the television spin-off *K9 and Company*.

The annuals are now remembered with affection by fans, even though the stories within often bore little resemblance to the television show. Rights issues would dog the annuals for many years, with little use made of the Doctor's on-screen foes, while companions would often bear no resemblance to their television counterparts.

The scarcity of the annuals varies; while the first was relatively common due to a high print run, the three annuals featuring Patrick Troughton were produced in much lower numbers and are now very hard to find. The first ever Jon Pertwee volume is the scarcest in the range. The remaining 1970s and 1980s annuals, while not commonplace, can still be found for reasonable prices.

The last World Distributors volume was released in 1985 (for 1986), when declining sales and uncertainty over the future of the television show led World to let their license lapse. As well as the annuals, World also published a number of one-offs, including *Invasion from Space*, which was a storybook featuring a single text story. There was also *The Amazing World of* Doctor Who: a mail-in book from Typhoo Tea, which

1960s *Doctor Who* annuals (World Distributors).

1970s *Doctor Who* annuals (World Distributors).

1980s *Doctor Who* annuals (World Distributors).

World also produced several specials that were not part of the normal run.

mainly reprinted the 1976 annual but also included some new material. World also published two bumper compilations: *An Adventure in Space and Time* and *Journey through Time*.

In the 1990s Marvel, publishers of the *Doctor Who Magazine*, picked up the license and produced a similar publication, titled the *Doctor Who Yearbook* – five volumes were issued in total.

Right: *Doctor Who Press-Out Book* (1978). One of several activity and colouring books from World Distributors.

Below: 1990s *Doctor Who* Yearbooks (Marvel).

The Dalek Pocket Book and *Space Travellers' Guide* (Souvenir Press, 1965).

The Making of Doctor Who (Piccolo, 1972).

Aside from the annuals and various activity books, the 1960s and early 1970s featured only a smattering of *Who*-related publications. Exploiting the Dalek bandwagon, the *Dalek Pocket Book and Space Travellers' Guide* was a paperback encyclopedia-style guide to the Daleks that featured a lot of biographical data on the creatures that had been invented for the book, much of which was ignored in future television episodes. *The Making of* Doctor Who, published by Piccolo in 1972 and written by the then script editor Terrance Dicks and television writer Malcolm Hulke, was the first ever book that went behind the scenes of the series. It featured a large section concentrating on the making of the story 'The Sea Devils'.

The first actual *Doctor Who* novel – *Doctor Who in An Exciting Adventure with the Daleks* – was published in 1964. This was an adaptation of the first ever television story featuring the Daleks. It was written by David Whitaker, who had been the programme's script editor during its first season and was one of the chief architects in the show's genesis.

As the book was intended as a standalone, it was rewritten as the first *Doctor Who* adventure, but with an opening somewhat at variance with the first ever *Doctor Who* episode 'An Unearthly Child'. It was initially released in hardback by Frederick Muller and was followed by two other adaptations of television stories: *The Zarbi* by Bill Strutton and *The Crusaders*, also by Whitaker. *The Daleks* and *The Crusaders* were later released as paperback editions, with different covers and internal illustrations.

No further novelisations were issued until 1973, when a newly formed children's label called Target Books acquired reprint rights to the three 1960s Frederick Muller titles. With striking new covers by artist Chris Achilleos, the books debuted in the series' tenth-anniversary year and were an instant success.

It was soon realised that more *Doctor Who* titles were needed and Target turned to the *Doctor Who* production office for suitable writers. Newly penned adaptations of several Jon Pertwee stories soon hit the market, and the trend through much of the 1970s was generally to adapt contemporary episodes with the occasional older adventure peppered in.

In the early years titles were often changed if the television title was not felt to be strong enough: 'Spearhead from Space' became *The Auton Invasion*, 'Robot' became *The Giant Robot* and 'Frontier in Space' became *The Space War*, to name a few.

While the range initially featured a wider repertoire of writers from the television show, as the books progressed Terrance Dicks found himself writing the lion's share of the titles. His friend Malcolm Hulke was also a regular contributor to the range until his death in 1979. Later, Ian Marter, who had played companion Harry Sullivan on television, became another prolific contributor. Dicks's output started to decline in the 1980s as Target gave first option on adapting stories to the original scriptwriters, and it was at this point that many new names started to appear on the book spines.

As the range progressed, the focus gradually began to shift to the older stories of the first two Doctors, mainly because the supply of recent television episodes to adapt began to dry up. There were various attempts to prolong the life of the book series, including *The Companions of* Doctor Who, which comprised two original books featuring Turlough and Harry Sullivan, and a novelisation of the *K9 and Company* television pilot. There was also *The Missing Episodes*, a three-book series adapting unmade scripts from the twenty-third season and novelisations of the audio stories *Slipback*, *The Pescatons* and *The Paradise of Death*.

The Target range is noted for its striking jacket artwork, which often made the stories look much more lavish than they had on television. Chris Achilleos handled the

Above: 1960s hardback novelisations
(Frederick Muller).

Left: *Doctor Who in an Exciting
Adventure with the Daleks* (Armada,
1965).

12–15

Right: *Doctor Who and the Crusaders* (Green Dragon, 1967).

Below: 1970s *Doctor Who* novelisations (Target).

1970s *Doctor Who* novelisations (Target).

bulk of the early covers; other notable contributors included Jeff Cummins, Andrew
Skilleter and Alister Pearson. Less well received were a short run of mid-1970s covers
rendered in a comic book style by Peter Brookes and a series of photographic covers
for many of the Peter Davison episodes. The covers were often painted, with little to
no reference material supplied, and use of various actor likenesses was often limited.
Despite sometimes being at variance with what was seen on television, this nevertheless
added to the creativity of the covers.

Many of the books, particularly the early titles, have been reprinted many times over
the years. In the 1970s and '80s, a new cover would occasionally be painted for a reissue,
while in the 1990s a majority of the reprints received new jackets. The books were also
issued in many foreign territories, often with new and wildly inaccurate artwork.

Hardback versions that were intended mainly for libraries were published under
the Allan Wingate and later WH Allen imprints. Initially only the *Auton Invasion* and
the *Cave Monsters* were released in hardback with most of the early '70s editions
with Chris Achilleos art being available in paperbacks only, and only receiving
hardback printings much later with different art. No Allan Wingate/WH Allen
hardcovers were ever issued for the Daleks or the Zarbi. From the mid-1970s
hardbacks were issued mostly in tandem with the paperbacks, but in later years
would be published around five months ahead. The hardbacks were halted in 1988
with the release of *The Smugglers* and the remainder of the range was available in
paperback only.

1980s *Doctor Who* novelisations (Target).

In the early 1980s a decision was made to number the books. All previously issued books were arranged in alphabetical order and these numbers would then appear on subsequent reprints; new books were then numbered based on their order of release.

Throughout the majority of the 1970s and '80s, the books had appeared on a regular, often monthly basis but through the early 1990s new titles became more sporadic. The last few adaptations dropped the Target logo from the covers entirely and only featured it on the interior pages. By the mid-1990s Virgin books, who had acquired the Target label, were successfully publishing original new *Doctor Who* fiction and the Target label was quietly retired. The last book bearing the Target logo was a reprint of *The Talons of Weng-Chiang*, released in 1994.

Sadly Target never did adapt the full run of classic *Doctor Who* television episodes. Rights and royalty issues prevented 'The Pirate Planet', 'City of Death', 'Shada', 'Resurrection of the Daleks' and 'Revelation of the Daleks' from being novelised. BBC books have since issued adaptations of 'The Pirate Planet', 'City of Death' and 'Shada', although the format and style is a far cry from the Target books of old.

As well as the novelisation range, Target also produced various non-fiction and activity books; notable examples included *The Doctor Who Monster Books*, the *Doctor Who Discovers* series of history books and the *Doctor Who Programme Guide*. Also released were two junior novelisations, wherein Terrance Dicks rewrote *The Giant Robot* and the *Brain of Morbius* for younger readers.

1990s *Doctor Who* novelisations (Target).

Above: Various spin-off novels (Target).

Right: *Doctor Who in an Exciting Adventure with the Daleks* (Avon books, 1967).

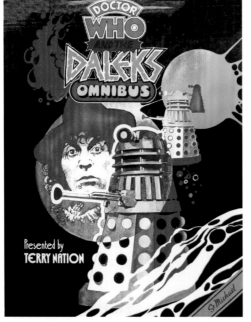

Above: These Japanese editions of the novelisations featured some highly unusual jacket artwork.

Left: *Dr. Who and the Daleks* Omnibus (St Martins Press, 1976). This large hardback, exclusive to Marks and Spencer, collected the novelisations of 'Planet of the Daleks' and 'Genesis of the Daleks'.

Junior *Doctor Who* novelisations (Target).

Various non-fiction paperbacks (Target).

Build the TARDIS (Target, 1987). Press-out pieces allowed you to assemble a cardboard TARDIS model.

In more recent times, Target books have gone through something of a renaissance with audiobook versions from the BBC as well as a select series of reprints.

Due to the sheer volume printed, estimated at over 8 million copies, Target books can still be picked up fairly easily, although condition is often variable. While many of the books from the first ten years were reprinted multiple times, from the mid-1980s the amount of reprints declined dramatically and titles that only had one print run are now among the hardest to find. *The Wheel in Space* is generally regarded as the rarest book in the range. As the hardbacks were printed in much lower numbers and were intended for libraries, they are much more difficult to find, especially in unmarked condition, and some of the early titles have been known to attract three-figure sums.

In today's age, where films and television shows can be relived instantly at the touch of a button, the novelisation has rapidly gone out of fashion, but for a generation Target books were almost as much a part of *Doctor Who* as the series itself.

While Target published the lion's share of *Doctor Who* books during the 1970s and 1980s, it was not unknown for other publishers to release titles. Magnet released a series of quiz books in the early 1980s, while *Doctor Who* got in on the rage for fantasy game books with a series of 'Make Your Own Adventure' books from Severn House. Six books were issued, all but one written by writers from the television series. Titan also published a number of script books.

K9 children's books (Sparrow, 1980).

WH Allen, who owned Target books, issued several large coffee-table books. *Doctor Who: A Celebration* was the first of these, published to celebrate the programme's twentieth anniversary, and further volumes quickly followed, mostly written by Peter Haining.

By the late 1980s Target had virtually exhausted the supply of television stories that could be turned into novels. After many years of vetoing the idea, the BBC finally gave permission for original stories to be published. By this point it was becoming clear that the series would be taking a prolonged break from television screens, and so it was

Aside from Target, several other publishers also issued *Doctor Who* paperbacks in the 1980s.

Doctor Who script books (Titan).

Various hardcover reference books.

Various softcover reference books.

decided that the original books, dubbed *The New Adventures*, would pick up the Seventh Doctor and Ace's adventures from the end of the last television story, 'Survival'.

Target had always been a children's book label and, although some of the later novelisations had become more lengthy and adult in nature, it was felt that *The New Adventures* should be published under a different label. It was intended that the books would be placed in the science fiction rather than children's section of book stores. Virgin books had acquired WH Allen in the late 1980s but *The New Adventures* were published under Virgin's newly formed *Doctor Who* books imprint.

From the outset it was decided to make the books progressive rather than just an exercise in nostalgia. As they were pitched at an adult audience, sex and bad language were allowed to be featured, which proved controversial with many fans.

Virgin had an open-door policy for submissions and, as a result, much of the range was penned by *Doctor Who* fans. Many of these names have since risen to prominence working on the television series itself, including Paul Cornell, Gareth Roberts and Mark Gatiss. While already an established writer, Russell T. Davies's first *Doctor*

The New Adventures novels (Virgin/*Doctor Who* books).

Who work was the *New Adventure* entitled *Damaged Goods*. Authors that had previously worked on the television series included Terrance Dicks, Marc Platt and Andrew Cartmel.

As the books progressed, new characters were dropped and introduced, much as they would have been on television. Bernice Summerfield, created as an initial replacement for Ace in the books, left a legacy that still continues today, with the character having featured in several spin-offs including her own audio series.

In 1996, when *Doctor Who* finally returned – albeit briefly – to television, the BBC opted not to renew Virgin's license and decided it would be more lucrative for their own book division to publish *Doctor Who*. With their license due to lapse the following year, Virgin, somewhat in defiance of the situation, decided that *The New Adventures* range would be strong enough to continue without the Doctor. The books would continue instead with Bernice Summerfield and other non-BBC copyright characters that had been specifically created for *The New Adventures*. To soften this transition the *Doctor Who* logo was dropped from the books from late 1996 onwards, even for the novels still under license featuring the Doctor. The *Bernice Summerfield New Adventures* were to run for only two years.

The New Adventures books are generally scarcer than the Target novelisations. Although the first few years' worth of titles can be had for reasonable prices, as the range progressed print runs declined and the later books are the hardest to find. The last three in the series – *Lungbarrow*, *The Dying Days* and *So Vile a Sin* – were only in stores briefly and nowadays command high prices.

The Missing Adventures novels (Virgin/*Doctor Who* books).

Various 1990s non-fiction paperbacks (Virgin/*Doctor Who* books).

While *The New Adventures* were being published, Virgin received many requests for novels featuring earlier incarnations of the Doctor. *The New Adventures* had always been conceived as a forward-looking series that would carry *Doctor Who* into new and uncharted waters. It was therefore decided to launch a second series that would tell all-new stories featuring the first six Doctors and these would be set in specific gaps between television stories.

Eighth Doctor and past Doctor novels (BBC Books).

Many of the writers from *The New Adventures* would work on the new range and, while the books aimed to capture the flavour of the era in which they were set, they were still approached in an adult vein, although were slightly more restrained than the sister series. The range featured several sequels to many popular television stories, including 'The Web Planet', 'Pyramids of Mars' and 'Talons of Weng Chiang'.

The Missing Adventures ran until 1997, when the expiration of Virgin's *Doctor Who* license brought the range to an end. As with *The New Adventures*, later *Missing Adventures* are much harder to find than the initial releases.

In 1997 BBC Books took over publishing *Doctor Who* novels, and two separate ranges were launched, one featuring the ongoing adventures of the Eighth Doctor, the other featuring the first seven Doctors. Unlike the Virgin novels, neither range had a subtitle. The books were authored by many of the same writers from *The New Adventures*. Both ranges wrapped up shortly after the television series returned to screens in 2005.

The new series has seen the amount of spin-off fiction go into overdrive. Although most of the books are related to the current series, occasional classic series titles continue to be released.

Doctor Who has probably spawned more books than any other television series in history and original novels featuring the character have had an unbroken twenty-five-year run. While the books will always be considered a spin-off to the series, it is humbling to think that the Doctor has had far more adventures on the printed page than he has had on television.

CHAPTER 2

Toys, Models and Games

Over the years *Doctor Who* has enjoyed a somewhat chequered relationship with the toy industry, with the series' peaks and troughs in popularity usually corresponding with the amount of toys on the market.

It is often argued the Daleks saved *Doctor Who* from obscurity and early cancellation. Certainly, without the Daleks the series merchandising during its first decade would have been vastly different, perhaps almost non-existent. When the Daleks made their television debut, toy manufacturers were quick to see the inherent marketing potential in the robot-like creatures and soon toy shelves were lined with a myriad of toy Daleks of all shapes and sizes.

Perhaps the most prolific Dalek toys were those produced by the Louis Marx company. The best known of the range was the battery-operated Dalek, also referred to as the 'Bump and Go Dalek', as, when it hits an obstacle, it turns and heads in the opposite direction. Measuring 6.5 inches, it was available in black and silver liveries and there were two unique packaging designs. Marx also sold the same basic Dalek with a friction drive mechanism, and also minus its working parts as a construction kit. The friction drive version was also available in a smaller 4.5-inch version.

Perhaps one of the more enduring *Doctor Who* toys, the Battery-Operated Dalek was re-released in red and yellow liveries with revised packaging in the 1970s and again in the 1990s as a limited edition by Dapol in a replica of the original packaging. The '90s version was available in black, silver, red and gold, and Dapol also reissued the friction drive version in various colours. Although inaccurate by today's standards, the toys were used briefly in model shots in a number of classic episodes. Marx also issued small 2-inch Daleks with a ball bearing in the base called 'Rolykins'.

Various Daleks put out by the Louis Marx company.

Left: Mechanical Dalek (Cowan De Groot, 1965).

Middle: Dalek Nursery toy (Selcol, 1965).

Right: Push Along Dalek (Herts Plastic Moulders, 1965).

The Dalek Oracle (Bell Toys, 1965).

Other notable '60s Dalek toys were the Mechanical Dalek, often referred to as the Clockwork Dalek, by Cowan De Groot and a Dalek model sometimes referred to as the Push Along Dalek from Herts Plastic Moulders which was sold as a Woolworths exclusive. Like the Marx Daleks, the Herts version was also to feature in the TV show and can be seen in the production line sequence in 'Power of the Daleks'.

Several Dalek games were released, the most notable of which was 'The Dalek Oracle', a variant of the popular Magic Robot game. A Dalek would be turned to point at a question and then be placed on the opposing side of the board where it would point to the answer. While this appeared magical to children, it was of course achieved by some carefully concealed magnets.

Some of the most sought after Dalek items today are the two different dressing up costumes. The first, by Scorpion Automotives, received a very limited release as much of the stock was destroyed in a fire. The second version by Berwick was more prolific, although due to the flimsiness of the PVC skirt it can be hard to find complete examples. For those children who would rather be blasting a Dalek than impersonating one, there was a line of anti Dalek guns from Lincoln International. In reality these were mostly pre-existing toys with slight modifications dressed up in Dalek packaging.

Left: Dalek Playsuit (Berwick, 1965).

Right: Anti Dalek Disintegrator (Lincoln International, 1965).

Doctor Who Give a Show Projector (Chad Valley, 1965).

The public's fascination with the Daleks meant that 1960s toys featuring other *Doctor Who* elements were very thin on the ground. Raphael Lipkin released a TARDIS money box, while Chad Valley released the *Doctor Who* Give a Show Projector set, which came packaged with sixteen slides featuring artwork telling a number of short *Doctor Who* stories. As well as featuring the Daleks the slides prominently featured the Zarbi and Menoptera from the television story 'The Web Planet'.

Following the success of the Daleks, the BBC always had their eye on other characters as the next big merchandising opportunity. It was hoped the Mechonoids, introduced as the Daleks' enemies in the story 'The Chase', would take off but only two toys were produced. Even the debut of the Cybermen, who soon replaced the Daleks as the show's recurring enemy during the latter half of the 1960s, wasn't enough to inspire any toys.

After the initial deluge of Dalek products during the mid-1960s, *Doctor Who* toys rapidly vanished from store shelves as children's appetites moved on to other popular television fads of the day, such as Batman and the various Gerry Anderson puppet series. The result was that no new toys were released during the whole of Patrick Troughton's tenure, and even Jon Pertwee's era, which saw the show regaining new success in the ratings, saw only a handful of jigsaws released. Even the Doctor's car *Bessie* wasn't enough to interest toy manufacturers!

The debut of Tom Baker in 1974 saw *Doctor Who* soar in popularity and it was at this point that toy companies began to sit up and take interest again. Probably the most popular *Who* toy of the 1970s was the Talking Dalek manufactured by TOMY and sold in the UK under the Palitoy/Bradgate brand. The Dalek measured 6.5 inches tall and uttered several phrases that were activated by a button on the top of the dome. It was available in red and silver liveries. The toy proved popular enough for Palitoy to follow it up with a Talking K9 a few years later.

One of the most sought-after *Doctor Who* collectables today are the dolls or action figures released by Denys Fisher. Measuring around 9 inches, the figures were produced in the then-popular Action Man style with fabric clothing. An initial five figures were released in the range: the Doctor, Leela, Cyberman, Giant Robot and Dalek. A TARDIS was also available, constructed from a durable cardboard and featuring a rotating drum on the interior that appeared to make the Doctor vanish. K9 was a late addition to the range after proving a popular addition to the television show. Despite a few inaccuracies, including a Cyberman with a nose and a rather diminutive Dalek, the figures are fondly remembered by many fans.

In boxed, complete condition, many of the figures now command several hundred pounds each. The Doctor and the TARDIS are the easiest to find, while Leela and the Dalek are the rarest. The Doctor figure was also released in Italy by Harbert and the toys also received Australian distribution by Toltoys.

Other notable *Who* toys released during the 1970s were two board games from Denys Fisher, one titled simply 'Doctor Who' and the other 'War of the Daleks'. There was also a *Doctor Who* dressing-up costume featuring a mask of Tom Baker and a PVC costume. This was sold in generic Superhero packaging that toy company Berwick used for all its various film and television character costumes.

Dubreq's Top Trumps was a popular card game in the 1970s and Jotastar got in on the action with a similar Trump card game themed around *Doctor Who*. Unusually, the heroes aside from the Doctor are not actually characters from the series but figures drawn from history, fiction and mythology. The set has a notorious blunder, with the Ogron and Sea Devil cards having their names mixed up.

Early 1970s jigsaws.

Left: Talking Dalek (Palitoy Bradgate, 1975).

Right: *Doctor Who* action doll – Italian release (Harbert, 1979).

Left: Leela action doll (Denys Fisher, 1977).

Right: Cyberman action doll (Denys Fisher, 1977).

Tardis playset (Denys Fisher, 1977).

Doctor Who board game (Denys Fisher, 1975).

War of the Daleks board game (Denys Fisher, 1975).

Doctor Who Trump Card game (Jotastar, 1978).

Another popular toy of the period was Viewmaster, and GAF released two *Doctor Who* sets covering the stories 'Full Circle' and 'Castrovalva'. The pictures were obtained by a photographer from Viewmaster, capturing images on a special stereoscopic camera during rehearsal sessions for the episodes. The 'Full Circle' slides were also available as a box set that included the camera.

Although the show was still enjoying good ratings, the debut of Peter Davison as the Fifth Doctor marked a decline in interest from toy manufacturers, with some jigsaws and a TARDIS tent being the only notable examples during this period. This drought would continue through the Colin Baker era, which too was sparsely represented on toy shelves.

While the high street was largely devoid of any *Doctor Who* toys during this period, there were actually decent quality models being produced, although these could be only obtained through mail order or through specialty stores such as Forbidden Planet. Sevans Models was run by *Doctor Who* fan Stuart Evans, who released a series of premium-priced construction kits. Unlike most model kits on the market, the kits were vacuum formed rather than injection moulded, which involved cutting the parts out of plastic sheets. Copious amounts of filler were needed to hide the joins. Despite the fact that these kits were not easy to make, with decent modelling skills very accurate replicas of the television characters could be achieved. The company's Dalek was even used for a short sequence in the 1985 story 'Revelation of the Daleks'. The company released various *Doctor Who* models over a number of years including an Earthshock Cyberman, Ice Warrior, Movie Dalek and Davros. Comet Miniatures were the next to release *Doctor Who* kits in the early 1990s, with a short series of kits comprising of movie and television Daleks and the Second and Fourth Doctors.

Enemies of *Doctor Who* jigsaws (Whitman, 1978).

Doctor Who Viewmaster
slides (GAF Corp).

Left: Tardis tent (Dekker, 1982).

Below: 1980s *Doctor Who* model kits (Sevans).

 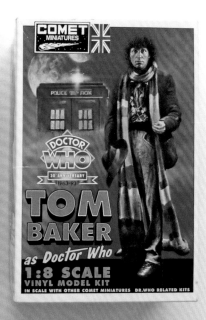

1990s *Doctor Who* model kits (Comet Miniatures/Amerang).

Star Wars figures, first released in 1978, had created a revolution in the action-figure industry, with a new solidly sculpted figure measuring approximately 3.75 inches tall becoming the predominant standard. In 1988 a UK company called Dapol, known for producing model railways, launched the first bona fide *Doctor Who* figures. The initial figures were mostly based around the then recently broadcast Seventh Doctor's debut 'Time and the Rani', but other characters from the show's history gradually began to appear. The Dapol range remains notorious to this day for its many inaccuracies, including a five-sided console, green K9 and a one-armed Davros.

New figures were produced at irregular intervals until 1990, when a decrease in interest following cancellation of the television series led to Dapol simply reissuing existing products for a few years. New figures resumed in 1996 and several new characters were released over the next few years among many reissues and variants. Figures came packaged either singly or sometimes in gift sets. As Dapol kept virtually all of their figures in production throughout the duration of their license, figures can be found in a variety of different packaging designs.

In 2000 the company switched to making immobile figures in a slightly larger scale, but only two of these were released before Dapol lost their license in 2002. For years the Dapol range was poorly regarded among *Doctor Who* collectors due to their rather outdated, simplistic design. Now the figures are becoming collectable and, although

25th anniversary playset (Dapol, 1988).

3.75-inch action figures (Dapol).

relatively few unique products were produced, there are a myriad of variants and different packaging designs for which the budding collector can search. Some of these were produced in very limited numbers for special events held at the Dapol factory, which for a time also housed the *Doctor Who* exhibition.

In the 1990s, with the television show off the air, aside from Dapol, toys were unsurprisingly sparse. The decade had little to offer the toy collector apart from a board game, a handheld LCD game and a Dalek playset.

Battle for the Universe
board game (The Games
Team, 1990).

Dr. Who and the Daleks LCD
game (Systema, 1993).

Dalek Playcase (Bluebird, 1998).

Talking figures (Product Enterprise).

By the early 2000s things were beginning to change, as action figures and toys were increasingly being made with an eye not on the children's market but on that for the adult collector. Product Enterprise tapped into the demand for nostalgia, issuing toys reminiscent of those from days gone by in retro packaging.

After releasing their own updated versions of the Marx Rolykins, there was a new take on the Talking Dalek that was somewhat more sophisticated than the Palitoy

Radio Control TV Dalek (Product
Enterprise, 2002).

model. A radio-control Dalek had first been mooted as far back as the 1960s, but
it took nearly forty years for the idea to become a reality. The Product Enterprise
remote-control television Dalek stood 12 inches tall and was released in many
different liveries, representing a majority of the television adventures. The sculpt was
later revised and issued as a movie Dalek from *Daleks' Invasion Earth 2150 A. D.* The
handset for the movie Dalek was modelled on the flying saucer from the film.

Other notable Product Enterprise items included Dalek Roll-a-Matics, Talking
Cyberman and Fourth Doctor figures, a remote-control Davros and an inflatable Dalek.

When *Doctor Who* returned to television in 2005, the BBC shopped it around
various toy companies, knowing that a new television launch could well spark a big
demand for related products. The master toy license was awarded to Oldham-based
Character Options. After having had huge success with action figures based on the
modern series, Character Options obtained the rights to produce figures based on the
classic series. The classics range has grown to represent all the original Doctors, nearly
all the Dalek and Cyberman variants and a good smattering of aliens and companions.

Only a few waves of figures were released to mass market; the majority were
produced in conjunction with Underground Toys as exclusives and mostly released
through the Forbidden Planet chain of stores.

The figures have been released in a variety of ways, ranging from single and double
packs to box sets with many themed around particular stories.

Radio Control Movie Dalek (Product Enterprise, 2006).

Infra Red Control Movie Dalek (Product Enterprise, 2005).

Right: Dalek
Roll-a-Matics
(Product
Enterprise, 2002).

Below: Micro
Talking Movie
Daleks (Product
Enterprise, 2006).

Left: Diecast figurines (Corgi, 2004).

Below: Doctor and Companions action figures (Character Options).

The initial 2008 series and the subsequent Age of Steel release came with build-a-figure components that enabled you to assemble either a K1 robot or a Cybercontroller if you collected all the figures in that wave. There have also been two series of Daleks with a talking feature, a fiftieth-anniversary series of Doctor and Daleks sets (exclusive to Toys R Us) and large boxsets featuring the Eleven Doctors and the Thirteen Doctors.

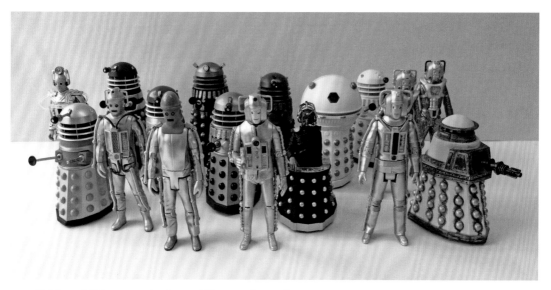

Daleks and Cybermen action figures (Character Options).

Villains and Monsters action figures (Character Options).

As many of the figures were released as exclusives, they were produced in numbers far lower than the new series range and are likely to become very collectable in the future. As of 2017 the number of new figures has slowed to a trickle, but odd variants and reissues continue to be released. A smaller 3.75-inch figure range was introduced by Character Options in 2013 to mixed opinions and a few classic Dalek designs were included.

Packaged examples of various *Doctor Who* figure sets (Character Options).

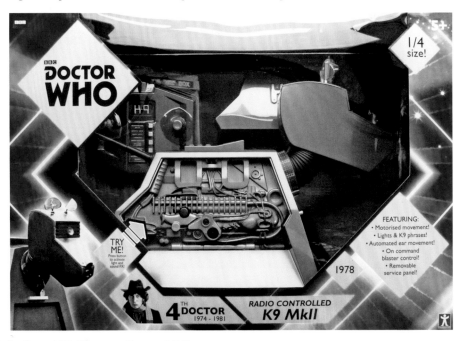

Radio Control K9 (Character Options, 2014).

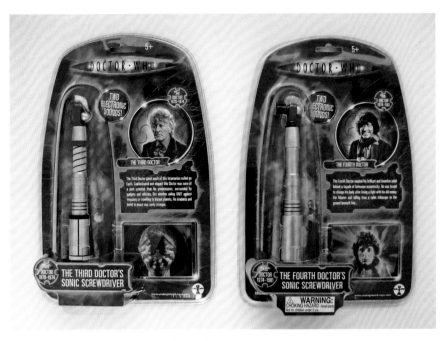

Electronic Sonic Screwdrivers (Character Options).

Doctor Who retro figures (Bif Bang Pow).

1/6 scale First and Fourth Doctor figures (Big Chief Studios).

As well as the more mainstream Character Options figures, there have been two other niche ranges of figures. Bif Bang Pow's retro figures were designed to ape the style of 1970s figures by Mego, who had contributed to the Denys Fisher range. Despite extensive plans, this range was cut short. Big Chief have more recently been producing high end 1/6-scale figures. Although primarily concentrating on the new series, the company has so far produced figures of the First and Fourth Doctors with plans for the rest.

The last few years have seen the amount of *Doctor Who* toys on the high street on the decline again as its 2000s child audience ages out of it. Nevertheless the series today is a globally recognised brand and, despite interest inevitably waxing and waning in the future, it is unlikely that *Doctor Who* toys will ever vanish completely from the market again.

CHAPTER 3

Audio Visual

It is easy to forget in today's world, where virtually any *Doctor Who* episode can be viewed at the touch of a button, that things weren't always that way. For the first two decades of its history experiencing an old *Doctor Who* episode was a rare experience; occasionally the BBC would repeat a story but generally, unless you were lucky to have taped the episodes off air, viewing an episode was a one-time-only experience.

Dr Who and the Daleks Super 8 Cinefilm (Walton, 1977).

Daleks Invasion Earth 2150 AD Super 8 Cinefilms (Walton, 1977).

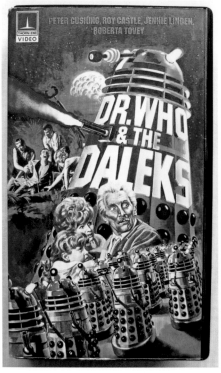

Dr Who and the Daleks rental video (Thorn EMI, 1982).

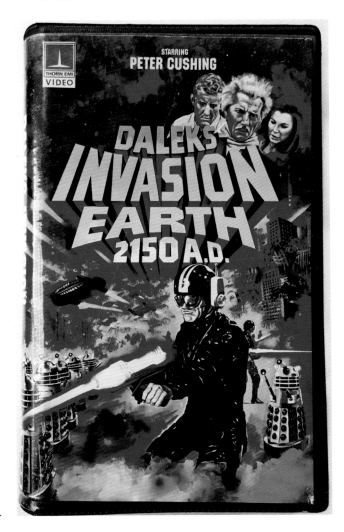

Daleks Invasion Earth 2150 AD
Rental video (Thorn EMI, 1982).

Ironically, during the 1960s and 1970s, the most accessible form of *Doctor Who* was the two feature films starring Peter Cushing. These occasionally appeared on television and were still played in cinemas as matinee fodder well into the late 1970s. The two films were also to be *Doctor Who*'s first fledgling steps into the home entertainment market.

Super 8-mm film, while mainly a popular format for making home movies, was also used as a medium to sell feature films for home viewing. Unfortunately, due to the high costs and large amount of reels involved, the medium never gained much leverage in the mass market and mainly catered to film enthusiasts and collectors. In 1977 Walton got in on the act with cine films of the movies *Dr. Who and the Daleks* and *Daleks' Invasion Earth 2150 A. D.* Each film was available in several formats: they could either be bought as a complete colour sound film split over eight reels or as a highly truncated version split over two reels. The two-reel version was available in both colour with sound and also as a cheaper black-and-white silent option. While the films can still be found on the secondary market, these are mainly the two-parters and complete eight-reel sets are very uncommon.

The two 1960s movies were also to be *Doctor Who*'s first entry onto the home video market. By the early 1980s, video rental was a growing phenomenon; for the first time the public could watch movies when and where they wanted, and video stores began to spring up in every neighbourhood. Naturally the primary interest was in new movies recently shown at the cinema but, as the market expanded, older films began to appear. Thorn EMI issued the two *Doctor Who* films in 1982 in both VHS and Betamax formats.

The sleeves featured striking new artwork covers by renowned movie poster artist Tom Chantrell; the *Dr. Who and the Daleks* art later featured on a poster released to video stores in the US. The movies were subsequently rereleased several times through the 1980s and 1990s at retail by Warner Home Video, although often featuring inferior cover designs.

It wasn't long before television companies began to see the potential in home video and the BBC launched their video arm in 1983. *Doctor Who* was an obvious choice to help spearhead the new venture and 'Revenge of the Cybermen' was chosen as the inaugural release. The episodes were edited together to form a feature-length movie and the cover strangely featured images of the Fourth Doctor and a Cyberman taken from totally different stories. The price was a colossal £39.99 for anyone who wished to purchase one. Due to the plethora of formats jostling for a share of the market, the story was released on VHS, Betamax and Video 2000.

The release did well enough for 'Brain of Morbius' to be issued the following year, although this was in a heavily abridged format. Further stories then continued to trickle out over the next few years, still primarily aimed at the rental market but slightly more affordable to the rich collector at the reduced price of £24.99 per tape.

By the mid-1980s, video tapes were beginning to be sold in high street stores rather than just rented and, at a cost of around £9.99 per tape, it was much more affordable for the average fan. Starting in 1986 the previously released *Who* tapes were gradually reissued at the new budget price in VHS format only. 1987 saw the first release exclusively on sell through, 'Death to the Daleks', and from this point on there were no further rental releases. Despite the *Who* tapes selling well, royalty and certification issues continued to be a minefield and no more than three stories a year were released till the end of the decade.

In 1990, the video range underwent something of a relaunch with artwork sleeves now replacing the previous photomontages and a regular release schedule saw on average two tapes arriving every couple of months. Stories were now released in their original episodic formats rather than the movie-length compilations that had mostly been the standard before. Eventually many of the earlier omnibus stories were rereleased in their episodic form. For stories with more than four parts, a release was usually split across two tapes, a controversial move with fans as many saw it as an excuse to charge double for a story that could have comfortably fitted on one tape. This practice was later phased out in the final years of the range with longer stories presented on one tape.

The range soon began to incorporate various special releases with new linking material. There were a series of tapes, each focusing on a particular Doctor's era. The first three Doctors' tapes were simply a collection of orphan episodes, while the Tom Baker and Colin Baker tapes featured the actors reminiscing over clips from their episodes. Despite plans Peter Davison and Sylvester McCoy tapes were never

'Revenge of the
Cybermen' rental
video (BBC, 1983).

recorded or released. Several incomplete stories were issued, with actors reading links or with photographic recreations set to audio. The legendary unfinished story 'Shada' finally saw the light of day, courtesy of the video range with Tom Baker narrating the missing segments. Several stories were also released as expanded editions with footage reinserted that had been cut from the original broadcasts. A majority of the special releases were supervised by ex-*Doctor Who* producer John Nathan Turner.

In 1996 the impending release of the *Doctor Who* television movie led to the range being put on temporary hiatus as shelves were cleared so that the movie would stand out. The film, which was part financed by BBC Enterprises with an eye on lucrative video sales, enjoyed the most high-profile launch of any *Doctor Who*

1980s videos (BBC).

title with midnight openings in some stores. An unfortunate delay in release, which saw it arriving only one week ahead of the television broadcast, resulted in sales not meeting expectations and a planned-for special edition was never released. The classic video range was relaunched later in 1996 with a rebranded look, and the artwork sleeves were soon phased out and replaced with digital photomontages, bringing a uniformity to all the BBC's *Doctor Who* output that also encompassed books and audio releases.

In 2003, twenty years after 'Revenge of the Cybermen' hit the shelves, the range finally came to an end with the release of a boxset containing the existing parts of the 'Reign of Terror' and three previously unreleased episodes from incomplete stories. For all of a few months *Doctor Who* fans could be content in the knowledge that they had a complete collection of every existing episode. Shortly after, however, the previously missing William Hartnell episode 'Day of Armageddon' was recovered and, over the years, a further eleven episodes have also found. These have since been released on DVD, which has left the video range an incomplete representation of the BBC's *Doctor Who* archive.

Early 1990s videos (BBC).

The rise of DVD as the preferred home entertainment format in the early 2000s led to subsequent mass purges by video collectors, with tapes thrown in landfill or donated to charity shops. As such many of the *Doctor Who* videos don't currently hold a great deal of collectable value. Nevertheless there is some sign of a pulse with original rental tapes starting to fetch reasonable prices, and it should be remembered that, as video slowly becomes an historical item, it is not inconceivable that in the future collectors will start to hanker over the nostalgia of big clunky tapes and the unique sleeve designs.

Towards the end of the 1990s, with the video range well established, there was a brief attempt to launch a rival format. Laserdisc offered a higher quality, more prestigious experience than video but never fully broke into the mainstream. BBC Video had previously dabbled in the format, releasing 'Revenge of the Cybermen' and 'Brain of Morbius' on laserdisc shortly after their original video releases. A couple of other stories had also been released overseas. All the BBC releases had been identical cuts to the video versions and featured the same sleeve images.

Late 90s/early 2000s videos.

The 1990s laserdiscs were licensed out to Encore Entertainment, who planned what was hoped would be an extensive range. Stories were released in episodic format over two large LP-sized discs, featuring all-new sleeve artwork. Sadly DVD was just emerging onto the market at the time and the range was cancelled after only three titles. Cover artwork is known to exist for an unreleased 'Spearhead from Space' release.

Doctor Who's inevitable arrival on DVD was a bit inauspicious, with a release of the 'Five Doctors' special edition, featuring a new edit of the story put together for video release a few years earlier. The release had little in the way of bonus material but did well enough to signal that there was interest in more *Doctor Who* in the fast-growing format.

The initial years of the range saw a slow roll-out of titles mainly focusing on the series classics. However, as DVD grew in popularity and the series returned to television in 2005, so the number of *Who* titles began to expand.

The remit of the DVD range was always to present the episodes in the best condition and as close to the original televised version as possible, and many new pioneering restoration techniques were used on the episodes. The DVD range was finally able to showcase the complete Jon Pertwee era in colour as well as restore a number of missing episodes to life by matching the off-air soundtracks to animation.

Video specials.

The release of 'The Underwater Menace' in 2015 meant that every episode of *Doctor Who* in the BBC archives was represented on DVD. Many fans assumed this was the end of the range but, in 2016, the BBC issued 'The Power of the Daleks' with all six of its missing episodes reconstructed with animation. Whether this leads to more missing or partially missing stories being released on DVD in this way remains to be seen.

Classic *Doctor Who* has also seen a small number of stories released on the high-definition Blu-ray format, including 'Spearhead from Space', *Doctor Who: The Movie* and 'Power of the Daleks'.

Like video before it, the market for DVDS and Blu-rays is declining rapidly due mainly to online streaming, downloads and subscription services such as Netflix. As all the UK BBC *Doctor Who* DVDs and Blu-rays are still in circulation at present, it is hard to assess any future collectable value. Nevertheless, it is likely that at some point titles will start to go out of print, which may lead to prices spiking if there is still a sufficient following for the physical format.

Nowadays it is easy to take for granted the fact that a *Doctor Who* fan can sit down to watch any existing episode wherever and whenever they want – forty years ago such a notion would have been as fanciful as travelling in the TARDIS itself.

1990s Laserdics (Encore Entertainment).

Doctor Who DVDs (BBC).

CHAPTER 4

Comics and Magazines

Today *Doctor Who* has no less than eight different ongoing publications in production by various companies – and yet, for the first sixteen years of its life *Doctor Who* had no regular title based on it. From 1964 *Doctor Who* appeared as a mainly black-and-white comic strip in *TV Comic*: a long-running publication from Polystyle featuring popular children's television characters. Many could be forgiven for thinking the Doctor was a poor relation as the Daleks also appeared in a comic strip; however theirs was a rather more prestigious affair, appearing in full colour in *TV21*, an anthology title mainly devoted to the various Gerry Anderson puppet series. After the Daleks were dropped from *TV21*, they began to feature in the *Who* strip in *TV Comic*. The *Doctor Who* strip ran in *TV Comic* until 1971, when Polystyle decided to move it into their all-new title *Countdown*, later to become *TV Action*, which featured slightly more sophisticated television-based strips. After *TV Action* folded, the *Doctor Who* strip returned to *TV Comic*, where it would remain until Polystyle relinquished their license in 1979.

Despite never publishing a regular title devoted to the series, Polystyle did produce three *Doctor Who* specials. Holiday specials were produced in 1973 and 1974, and

Various 1970s specials (Polystyle).

a winter special in 1977. The latter featured reprints of various Third Doctor strips with Tom Baker's likeness drawn over it, a cost-saving measure Polystyle had begun employing during the final years of the strip. Due to the flimsiness of the paper used, the specials are now very hard to find in decent condition. Also given away free with issue 1292 of *TV Comic* was the *Mighty Midget Doctor Who* comic, a sixteen-page issue featuring more overdrawn strips.

Radio Times tenth and twentieth anniversary specials (BBC).

1970s poster magazines (Legend/Harpdown).

Aside from the Doctor's appearances in Polystyle publications, there were a few other scant titles published by companies during the 1970s. 1973 was *Doctor Who*'s tenth anniversary and to mark the occasion *Radio Times* published a special. For the time this was a prestige publication and featured specially shot spreads featuring many actors from the series. In the absence of detailed information on the series at the time, this would also serve as a *Doctor Who* fan's bible for many years. Ten years later a second *Radio Times* special was released to commemorate the twentieth anniversary.

Two one-off poster magazines were also released in the mid-1970s, both by Legend/Harpdown Publishing, who also published similar titles on *Horror* and *Space: 1999*.

Towards the end of the 1970s, Dez Skinn, editorial director of the UK division of Marvel comics, began to see the potential in a title dedicated solely to *Doctor Who*. He had previously edited a Hammer Horror title that featured a mix of articles and comic strips, and thought a similar format would work well for *Doctor Who*. With Polystyle relinquishing their *Who* comic strip rights in early 1979, the way was clear for Marvel to launch a *Doctor Who* title.

Doctor Who Weekly launched in October of 1979 at the princely sum of 12p. The title was aimed primarily at children but acknowledged the series' older fan base with some articles looking back at the early years of the series. The comic strip, initially written and drawn by Pat Mills and John Wagner, was head and shoulders above the somewhat-dated stuff Polystyle had been offering in *TV Comic* and the style of Marvel's *Who* strip owed a little to the popular *2000 AD* comic that had launched a few years earlier. The magazine sold strongly on its launch, which coincided with the television series' seventeenth season; however, after a while, sales begun to lag and after forty-three weekly issues it was felt that the only way to save the publication would be to go monthly.

Initially the changes were negligible, with *Doctor Who Monthly* simply being a bumper version of the weekly, but gradually the tone of the magazine began to change,

Doctor Who Weekly magazines (Marvel).

Early 1980s *Doctor Who Monthly/Magazine* (Marvel).

with Marvel realising that the main audience for the magazine was teenagers and young adults rather than children.

From issue 85 the publication became known as the *Official Doctor Who Magazine*; however, the 'official' tag was later dropped and *Doctor Who Magazine* remains the title to this day. Over the years the publication has seen many changes in tone and format. Nevertheless constants over the years have been the news feature 'Gallifrey Guardian', a letters page and the comic strip. During much of the 1980s and early 1990s, *Doctor Who* producer John Nathan Turner vetted all content, which often meant coverage of certain aspects of the series was off bounds. Many *Who* fans increasingly turned to fan magazines for more in-depth content and, realising this, *DWM* began to recruit some of these writers themselves.

In 1995 Marvel UK was purchased by Panini publications, although the Marvel logo continued to appear on the magazine for a number of years. The 2005 relaunch of *Doctor Who* saw a major format change, with the publication becoming perfect bound and the page count expanding. In 2016 the magazine clocked up a record breaking 500 issues; having run uninterrupted since 1979, it can actually claim to have run longer than the series on which it is based.

Issues over the years have often come with a variety of free gifts, ranging from posters and postcards to audio CDs. Issues with the gifts intact are more collectable; the first four issues came with transfers, which are often missing or have been rubbed down onto the magazine.

As well as the regular monthly magazines, there have also been many special issues. Initially these were mainly reprints of material that had appeared in the regular title but, over the years, they have expanded into comprehensive guides on various aspects of the series. Also of note was a compilation of the Dalek comic strips from *TV21* and a one-off comic special called *Age of Chaos*, written by Colin Baker.

Late 1980s/early 1990s issues of *Doctor Who Magazine* (Marvel).

Late 1990s–present issues of *Doctor Who Magazine* (Marvel/Panini).

In America *Doctor Who* had enjoyed a fairly low profile until the late 1970s. Dell Comics had released a comic adaptation of the *Dr. Who and the Daleks* movie in 1966, which was published as part of their movie classics range, but it wasn't until the Tom Baker episodes caught on with audiences that interest warranted the launch of a US *Who* comic. The Marvel UK *Doctor Who* strip had always been planned with an eye

Various *Doctor Who Magazine* special issues (Marvel/Panini).

Dr. Who and the Daleks comic adaptation (Dell, 1966).

1980s US comics (Marvel).

Doctor Who Adventure comics (Golden Wonder/Marvel, 1986).

to it being reprinted in America and it made its stateside debut in 1981 over four issues of Marvel Premiere, a title dedicated to showcasing new characters. It would take another few years before it was felt that *Doctor Who* could support its own standalone title, with *Doctor Who* 1 debuting in 1984. The title was marketed as one of Marvel's prestige titles and was printed on better quality paper than regular Marvel fare, but carried a higher cover price and was sold only in comic stores. As with the Marvel Premiere issues, the title featured recoloured strips from *Doctor Who Weekly* and later *Doctor Who Monthly*. The odd article unique to the comic also appeared occasionally. The comics featured all-new cover art by Dave Gibbons. The title ran for twenty-three issues.

In 1986 a set of six mini comics were given away free in multipacks of Golden Wonder crisps; the comics featured colourised Sixth Doctor strips from *Doctor Who Magazine*.

Despite no series having been on the air for three years, Marvel UK took the revolutionary step of launching a second *Doctor Who* title in 1992. *Doctor Who*

Doctor Who Classic comics (Marvel).

Doctor Who Poster Magazines (Marvel).

Classic Comics was a showcase for the back catalogue of strips produced by Polystyle over the years, the rights to which had recently been acquired by Marvel. Issues contained a mix of strips featuring various Doctors, including some from the Marvel era. Where pages were originally in black and white, these were newly colourised. The title also featured articles on the history of the strip. Although the title reprinted all the Third Doctor strips included in regular issues of *Countdown* and *TV Action*, it featured only a cross-section of the strips from *TV Comic* which had featured the first Four Doctors. The title ran for twenty-seven issues, and a special entitled *Evenings Empire* was also produced, featuring a completed version of a story that had only been partially run in *Doctor Who Magazine*.

In 1994 Marvel launched a third *Doctor Who* title, the short-lived *Doctor Who Poster Magazine*, which ran for only eight issues, with a format change from issue 7 in an attempt to buoy sales.

The new series has spawned a whole new wave of magazines, including *Doctor Who Adventures*, *Battles in Time*, *Monster Invasion*, *Doctor Who Insider*, *Doctor Who DVD Files* and the *Doctor Who Figurine Collection*, all of which periodically feature content on the original series.

Doctor Who comics for the American market have also been published by IDW and Titan, which have featured appearances from older Doctors. Titan have also published several miniseries featuring the Classic Doctors.

Things have changed a lot from the early days, when a single company would control the comic and publication rights; now the BBC is content to split the licence across various companies. With such a plethora of titles, a *Doctor Who* fan is spoilt for choice these days. While in the 1960s, 1970s and 1980s it was easy to be a completist, today fans are more likely to pick and choose which titles they buy.

CHAPTER 5

Sound

Doctor Who has a long history of audio products on record, tape and CD. A 7-inch single release of the *Doctor Who* theme tune in 1964 was in fact the first ever piece of bona fide *Doctor Who* merchandise. In the 1960s there were no videos and only a handful of books, but one episode could be experienced over and over thanks to being released on vinyl. Titled *The Daleks* and released by Century 21 records, this was actually a recording of the final episode of the 1965 story 'The Chase'. Narration was provided by David Graham, who had been one of the Dalek voices on television.

Aside from further rereleases of the theme tune as a single and various unlicensed novelty records, there was then a sizeable gap until the release of *Doctor Who and the Pescatons* from Argo Records in 1976. This was an all-new partially dramatised story, featuring Tom Baker and Elisabeth Sladen, by Victor Pemberton who had written 'Fury from the Deep' for the show several years earlier. Initially released on vinyl only it was rereleased in the 1980s on both vinyl and cassette. Further CD reissues followed in the 1990s and 2000s, and the story was rereleased on vinyl again in 2013. The differing cover images utilised for the various releases feature conflicting depictions of the actual Pescaton creatures.

The Daleks mini album (Century 21 Records, 1966).

Doctor Who and the Pescatons LP (Argo Records, 1976).

BBC records released the *Doctor Who Sound Effects* LP in 1978. This collection of tracks was drawn mostly from the first four Tom Baker seasons and is interesting due to the fact that the sleeve notes refer to several stories by their working titles. Many purchasers at the time must have been baffled by the reference to non-existent stories such as 'The Destructors' and 'The Enemy Within'.

One of the most notable *Doctor Who* audio releases was the *Genesis of the Daleks* LP in 1979. This was an abridged version of the story's soundtrack with narration provided by Tom Baker. As such it was the first *Doctor Who* story to be made commercially available by the BBC. The initial release was available on 12-inch vinyl and cassette. It has subsequently been rereleased several times over the years on both cassette and CD, and has more recently been made available on vinyl once more.

Tom Baker's narrating abilities were put to use again shortly after, when Pickwick released a talking-book version of 'State of Decay'. Although written by Terrance Dicks, this was not a reading of the Target book which had not yet been published but a different

Doctor Who Sound Effects LP (BBC Records, 1978).

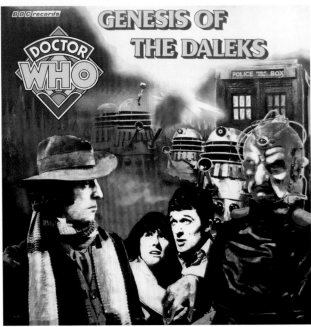

Genesis of the Daleks LP (BBC Records, 1979).

telling. The story was initially released as a single cassette mounted on a backing card before later being rereleased over two cassettes packaged in an outer card sleeve.

To mark the twentieth anniversary, BBC Records issued *Doctor Who: The Music*, which featured a collection of music suites from the series mainly drawn from then recent episodes. This was followed in 1985 by *Doctor Who: The Music II*, which featured incidental music from the twentieth and twenty-first seasons. Both titles

State of Decay Talking Book
(Pickwick, 1981).

Doctor Who: The Music (BBC Records, 1983).

were released on vinyl and cassette and were later made available on CD in the 1990s, retitled *Earthshock* and *The Five Doctors*. The *Doctor Who 25th Anniversary Album* followed in 1988 on vinyl, cassette and CD, and featured suites from the twenty-fourth series of the programme.

When *Doctor Who* disappears from television screens, it is often not long before an audio version appears to take its place, with the medium being significantly cheaper to produce than its visual counterpart. The first of these occasions was in 1985 when, following the announcement that the show was going on hiatus, a six-part story called 'Slipback' appeared on Radio 4 starring Colin Baker and Nicola Bryant. This received a belated cassette release in 1988, paired with the 1979 soundtrack version of 'Genesis of the Daleks'. The story was issued individually on CD in 2001.

In 1993 *Doctor Who* returned to radio again for its thirtieth anniversary with Jon Pertwee recreating the role alongside several of his fellow cast members. This was followed in 1996 by a sequel, 'The Ghosts of N Space', and both stories were released on cassette to tie in with their broadcasts, later to be issued on CD in the 2000s.

Doctor Who, like many British shows of the 1960s, has a large number of missing episodes, with the original masters long since disposed of as they were once deemed to be of no commercial use. The rarity of video-recording technology in the 1960s meant that there was little opportunity for the average viewer to record the visual aspect of the episodes, but far cheaper and more prevalent was audio recording and, over the years, off-air audio recordings of varying quality have been discovered of all the missing episodes.

These first saw commercial release on cassette in the early 1990s with 'Evil of the Daleks', 'Power of the Daleks', 'Fury from the Deep' and the 'Macra Terror' released, featuring linking narration that was provided by Tom Baker and Colin Baker. 'Tomb of the Cybermen' was also planned as part of this range, with narration by Jon Pertwee, and, although it was eventually released, the full story had been recovered and released on video by this point.

After a gap of several years the BBC picked up the idea again and began releasing missing audio stories on CD. The first of these, 'The Massacre', was also released on cassette but further releases were CD only. The missing episode CDs featured remastered soundtracks with the audio sometimes pulled from a variety of sources to achieve the best transfer. New linking narration was provided by various companion actors who had appeared in the original productions. All the missing episodes were released in this format, although subsequently several have been found or been

Doctor Who radio cassettes (BBC).

Missing episodes cassettes and CDs (BBC).

Among the many Big Finish productions *Doctor Who* audio plays are adaptations of the stage plays and unproduced TV stories.

animated for DVD release. Following the completion of the missing episodes CDs, the BBC also began releasing the audio soundtracks to selected existing stories with narration.

After many years of unofficial fan productions dabbling in the idea of *Doctor Who* stories produced exclusively for audio, including some featuring original actors from the series, Big Finish Productions were granted the licence to produce *Doctor Who* adventures on audio in 1999. These were released initially on cassette and CD, although cassettes were dropped after the first few releases. Initially featuring the Fifth, Sixth and Seventh Doctors, alongside their various assistants, the stories were written mainly by established fan writers, many of whom had worked on the Virgin and BBC novels.

Paul McGann's Eighth Doctor soon joined the range, followed eventually by Tom Baker's Fourth Doctor. During the eighteen years the range has been in production, it has grown into a behemoth with over 200 numbered main releases alongside numerous spin-offs featuring various Doctors, elements from the series such as Daleks, Cybermen and UNIT, adaptations of books, unmade television stories and stage plays. In any month alone there are usually no less than three *Doctor Who* productions from Big Finish.

Until 2015 every release was kept in print by Big Finish, but many of the older releases are now being allowed to go out of print and are available as downloads only, which may lead to values spiking in the future.

While the mainstream television viewer may be blissfully unaware of it, *Doctor Who* has enjoyed a parallel life in sound, with the amount of audio stories outnumbering the Doctor's television adventures. Should the series disappear from television screens again, it is likely that the audio adventures will continue unabated, keeping the flame alive.

CHAPTER 6

Cards

Doctor Who has over the years spawned a number of collectable card items, ranging from promotional giveaways to postcards, and in more recent times, lavish trading card sets aimed at the dedicated collector.

Although losing favour in recent decades due to their negative connotations, cigarette cards have been a part of British culture since the late nineteenth century. A series of *Doctor Who* cards were issued in 1964 by Cadet in packs of their *Dr. Who and the Daleks* sweet cigarettes. The set consisted of fifty cards, which told a story. As well as the Daleks, the cards featured the Voord from the 'Keys of Marinus'. A couple of years later a similar series of cards were issued and included with Wall's Sky Ray ice lollies. The set consisted of thirty-six cards, once again telling a loose story. An album into which the cards could be stuck was also sold in stores, and this doubled as an activity book. On both the cards and the album the Doctor was drawn as a strange of hybrid of the Hartnell and Troughton incarnations.

Daleks sweet cigarette cards (Cadet, 1964).

Doctor Who Adventure book (Walls, 1967).

The next *Doctor Who* cards were a well-remembered set from Weetabix in 1975. These featured artwork depictions of the Fourth Doctor, Sarah Jane Smith and various foes. These were given away in strips of four in Weetabix boxes and the idea was that the character could be pressed out of the card to make a stand-up figure. Dioramas were also printed on the backs of the Weetabix boxes.

Cards from the first *Doctor Who* promotion (Weetabix, 1975).

The success of this promotion led to Weetabix releasing a second set of cards in 1977. This time the cards took the form of game cards with four different boards provided on the back of the Weetabix boxes. Once again the cards came in strips of four, with one of the cards on the strip containing a secret message which could be translated using a decoder sheet included inside the boxes.

Cards from second *Doctor Who* promotion (Weetabix, 1977).

The Amazing World of Doctor Who poster and cards (Typhoo, 1976).

Doctor Who greeting cards (Denis Alan Print, 1979).

1980s *Doctor Who* postcards (BBC).

Doctor Who customisable card game (MMG, 1996).

1976 saw a set of twelve photographic cards released in packs of Typhoo Tea; these were part of a promotion titled 'The Amazing World of *Doctor Who*', with Typhoo offering an annual-style book for sale that came with a poster of the cover art, on to which the cards could be affixed.

If you were of a certain age in the late 1970s, you may have been the recipient of a *Doctor Who* birthday card. Eighteen in total were issued by Denis Alan print, featuring specially taken pictures of Tom Baker and the TARDIS.

During the 1980s a large number of *Doctor Who* character postcards were made available and sold through the BBC *Doctor Who* exhibitions as well as being sent out for free by fans writing into the *Doctor Who* production office. These were occasionally supplied signed by contemporary cast members and were also used by actors from the series to answer fan mail.

During the 1990s customisable card games with trading cards that actually featured as part of a game began to take off in popularity and, in 1996, a *Doctor Who* game was released to cash in on the craze. MMG released a *Doctor Who* set comprising 302 cards, released in either nine-card boosters or sixty-card starter decks. Cards were released in four rarity levels: Common, Uncommon, Rare and Ultra Rare. The three ultra rare cards released were Davros, the Fourth Doctor and the Doomsday Weapon, and these are hard to track down.

1990s *Doctor Who* trading cards (Cornerstone Communications).

While *Doctor Who* had appeared on trading cards previously in the form of promotional giveaways such as the Typhoo cards, the show had never before had its own dedicated trading card set. Cornerstone Communications issued the first *Doctor Who* trading card series in 1994. The cards were aimed firmly at the speciality market and came in packs of ten cards, with thirty-six packs to a display box. Cornerstone released four *Who* sets over a number of years. The first three releases combined to make a mammoth 330-card set. Various chase cards and autographs were also randomly inserted in packs. The fourth set was a standalone 120-card set printed on glossier stock than the first three sets. Various binders were also produced to hold the cards.

Strictly Ink picked up the *Doctor Who* trading card license in 2000 and released five sets over the next few years. Although treading similar ground to the Cornerstone releases, the cards featured an impressive autograph line-up, with cards featuring signatures from every surviving main cast member at that point, along with those of various guest stars and behind the scenes personnel.

Strictly Ink also obtained the license from Studio Canal for the 1960s *Doctor Who* films and released a set titled *Big Screen Doctor Who* along with a follow-up titled *Big Screen Additions*. The sets featured autographs from the whole of the surviving cast from both movies.

Above: *Doctor Who* trading cards (Strictly Ink).

Right: *Doctor Who* autographed trading cards (Strictly Ink).

In 2014 Strictly Ink, under a new moniker, Unstoppable Cards, released a further *Doctor Who* movie set.

Since 2006 various card sets have been released for the new *Doctor Who* series, and some of these have featured classic series content. The most notable of these was G. E. Fabbri's *Doctor Who Battles in Time*, a card game aimed at the younger fan that produced a set called 'Ultimate Monsters', which consisted mainly of classic series foes.

Doctor Who trading card binders (Strictly Ink).

CHAPTER 7

Collectors' Items

Until the 1980s there was really no such thing as the *Doctor Who* collectable. Most products were produced cheaply for a mass market audience with little thought given to any sort of longevity or potential value they may attain. It was precisely because of this disposability that much of the merchandise from the early days of the show is now so sought after. However, as its fan base matured and had a larger disposable income, manufacturers realised that higher priced, better quality product could be produced, aimed purely at the *Doctor Who* devotee.

One of the first companies to aim product at the collector base was Fine Art Castings, a company known for wargaming minatures. Having acquired the *Doctor Who* licence they released a number of pewter figurines over several scales. The largest was the 80-mm range, followed by a more affordable 40-mm range and a short-lived 25-mm scale. The figurines could be bought in various forms, either unpainted, antiqued finish or painted. A fair range of characters from the series was produced before Fine Art castings ceased production on the range in the mid-1980s.

Fine Art Castings also produced a range of Doctors and villains busts with a limited edition of 2,000, for which a plinth was provided if the full set was purchased.

Around the same time Royal Albert began issuing limited-edition plates of Doctors and villains. In the event, despite plans for all the Doctors to be represented, only plates for the first three Doctors were produced, while Roger Delagdo's Master and Davros were the only villains plates released.

Doctor Who Doctors bust set (Fine Art Castings, 1985).

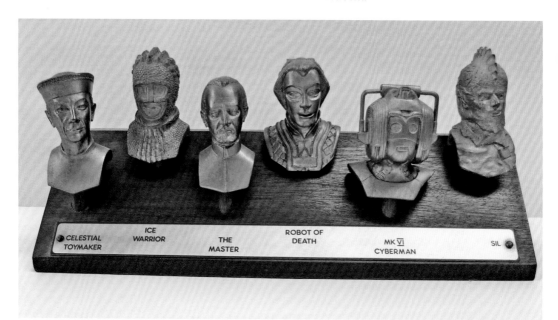

Doctor Who Villains bust set (Fine Art Castings, 1986).

Doctor Who bone china plates (Royal Albert, 1984).

1990s *Doctor Who* chess set and expansion (MBI).

Classic moments statues (Product Enterprise, 2001).

Doctor Who cookie jars (Cards Inc. Characters).

'The Master and Auton'
statue (Weta, 2010).

One of the more sought-after items today was the *Doctor Who* chess set, produced by MBI and released in 1992. The initial set consisted of thirty-eight pewter pieces, available by subscription only, and released at the rate of two every two months. This was followed by an expansion set featuring more companions and villains and by a final set of four, featuring characters from the 1996 *Doctor Who* television movie. The figures from the expansion sets are now much harder to find than the earlier base figures.

There have been various attempts over the years to launch ranges of *Doctor Who* statues, but sadly none have really taken off and releases usually judder to a halt after the first few products. Product Enterprise launched a series of classic moments statues in 2001, which comprised two dioramas representing 'An Unearthly Child' and 'The Tomb of the Cybermen' plus four monster figurines. There were also two larger 12-inch statues of the First and Second Doctors. Product Enterprise later reformed into a company known as Sixteen 12 collectibles, another statue range was unveiled in a 12-inch scale and a fair few prototypes of various monsters were unveiled, in the

The Fourth Doctor maxi bust
(Titan merchandise, 2012).

event however only the Fourth Doctor, and 'Revenge of the Cybermen' Cyberleader and Cyberman statues were released. A series of collectable cookie jars were released in the mid-2000s by Cards Inc characters. A Tardis, K9, Davros and Cyberman head were produced along with Daleks in various liveries.

Weta, the special effects company known for its work on *The Lord of the Rings* films, released a series of large 12-inch statues in 2009, capturing scenes from certain stories, and two hailed from the classic series: 'The Master and Auton', and 'Fourth Doctor and Davros'.

An increasingly popular collectable over the last couple of decades is the mini bust – a statue highlighting the upper torso of a character. Titan Merchandise released a *Doctor Who* range dubbed Maxi Busts but, despite plans for a more comprehensive range, only three classic series characters have been released: the Third and Fourth Doctors, and a Cyberman.

Unlike *Star Wars*, *Doctor Who* boasts few iconic handheld props; however, the series' most ubiquitous prop, the sonic screwdriver, surprisingly went totally

Sonic Screwdriver replica (Sixteen Twelve collectables, 2009).

un-merchandised for many years. The market is now playing catch-up and has been flooded with sonics of all shapes and sizes. The finest, however, was a limited-edition replica of the of Fourth Doctor's sonic screwdriver from Sixteen Twelve Collectables, made from metal and housed in an attractive display case.

It is fair to say that *Doctor Who* now caters to every type of collector: from cheap pocket-money toys to full-size props, the fan is spoilt for choice.

Afterword

If you have bought this book, chances are you already have some *Doctor Who* memorabilia, whether it's a few DVDs or books or a Tardis filling hoard.

A *Doctor Who* collection can be anything you want; having been a collector for over thirty years, my own collection has seen many changes and refinements.

The simple truth of collecting is, unless you are blessed with unlimited finances and space, it is impossible to own everything. Literally thousands of items have been produced since 1963, and nowadays the flow of monthly items is such that a second mortgage would be needed to keep up with it all.

A good tip for assembling a collection is to have some focus. It may be that you just want to collect Daleks, or maybe the toys or DVDs, but buying anything just because it says *Doctor Who* on it or because you've picked it up cheap isn't going to be the foundation to a great collection. It's very easy to fall into the trap of just collecting for the sake of it. The best rule of collecting is to buy what you like and gives you a buzz.

Today there is a plethora of sales channels available to the potential buyer. In some ways looking for that rare item is easier than ever. Thirty years ago, few *Who* products were available on the high street and in those distant prehistoric times before the internet, there was little choice but to order those elusive items by mail order or visit a specialty store or convention.

The advent of sites such as eBay has levelled the playing field somewhat in that there is much more collectable product out there than there ever was. An item that previously may have taken you years to find in the wild may now have several examples for sale online. The flip side is that sometimes you may have to pay over the odds; auctions are a good way of seeing an item attaining its true value, but there are many sellers who use the buy it now option and often flagrantly overcharge on the off chance that someone will pay it.

As anyone can sell on sites such as eBay and Amazon, some sellers will undoubtedly have higher standards than others. Don't be afraid to ask questions if a listing doesn't make things clear. Has the seller neglected to mention that that annual has been written in or that vintage toy has reproduction parts? Also, if a seller doesn't make clear how an item will be packaged, be sure to ask for reassurance. You really don't want to pay good money for an item only for it to arrive looking like it's been through a mangle. Most online sellers are honest and reliable, but when things go wrong it can be a very frustrating experience.

In the age of the internet it is often easy to forget there is such a thing as the high street, and many towns now have comic book and speciality stores who may stock *Who* items. There are also an increasing amount of collectors' fairs springing up around the country. It is definitely much easier to see an item in person and be immediately able to assess the condition. Condition is entirely subjective and things that may irk one collector may not be an issue to another. There is also little choice but for leniency with older items.

Once you have begun a collection, a big question is how it should be displayed. I strongly believe that the whole point of a collection is to see it and admire it; to that end storage and display are paramount. For magazines and comics, storage boxes obtainable from most comic shops are ideal. Three-dimensional items are more of a challenge, particularly bulky boxed items such as board games that weren't made with display in mind. Ikea, however, do some reasonably priced glass cabinets that are ideal for action figures and models. With some thought and effort a collection can look really impressive. It can also be handy to give items that bit of extra protection, as even stored in the best of environments, items can age and degrade. Books and magazines can be stored in acid-free bags available in comic stores; these sort of bags also come in handy for carded action figures and smaller items, helping guard against casual wear and tear.

A common topic among collectors is whether an item should be opened or left in its original packaging. This could be removing shrink wrap from a DVD, taking a toy from its blister or even cutting a piece of tape sealing a box. The truth is that anything which alters an item from its original manufactured state will have some bearing on value. But at the same time some perspective is needed; would a collection of shrink wrapped DVDs give you any pleasure? Will you get any satisfaction from owning a sealed Dalek figure that you can never touch? It's entirely the choice of the collector but do what makes you happy rather than worrying about potential investment; the market is so volatile that future collectability just can't be predicted.

With an influx of new collectors over the last ten years, collecting *Doctor Who* memorabilia is these days bigger than ever and items which were once seen as a relic of the past are now being enjoyed by a whole new generation. As one of Britain's most merchandised brands and a top earner for the BBC, *Doctor Who* collecting looks set to be with us for a long time to come.